BioGeometry Signatures Mandalas Coloring Book

Book cover design by Argenis Gil
Printed by CreateSpace

BioGeometry Signatures
Mandalas Coloring Book

What are BioGeometry Signatures?

BioGeometry Signatures are a special branch of the science of BioGeometry: a new field of science that uses specially designed shapes, color, sound, motion and wave configuration, to induce harmony into biological subtle energy systems. BioGeometry was founded by Dr. Ibrahim Karim and is based on over 45 years of research. Dr. Ibrahim Karim, an architect by profession, was intrigued by the function of shapes and the effect of earth energy locations on all living systems; this resulted in the birth of the science of BioGeometry. Based on his research on the power of shapes, Dr. Karim discovered a profound relationship between the shape of the body's organs and their internal energy flow patterns. One way to picture these patterns is by visualizing the energy flow within the human body as found in the Chinese Meridian system and then tracing these similar pathways within each organ. These energy flow patterns were the basis of an extensive body of research since the 1960s and were coined BioGeometry Signatures or BioSignatures for short.

BioGeometry Signatures are linear diagrams that help harmonize the subtle energy patterns of body organs. The organ subtle energy patterns are accessed through BioGeometry Signatures placed externally in the body's energy field to create a connection through Resonance of Shape, or through tracing the movement of the BioGeometry Signatures.

BioGeometry Signatures and the science of BioGeometry are not a form of medical diagnosis or treatment. They are a long-term environmental support for the body's energy system and all types of treatment.

To learn more about BioGeometry and BioGeometry Signatures the books *Back to a Future for Mankind, BioGeometry*, and *BioGeometry Signatures, Harmonizing the Body's Subtle Energy Exchange with the Environment* by Dr. Ibrahim Karim are available on Amazon.com

Heart

Stomach & Intestines

Thymus

Jaw & Tooth

Pineal Gland

General Balance & Relaxation

Lungs

Spine I

Adrenal Glands

Liver

Blood Vessels

Chakras

Tailbone Compression

General Balance II
Angelic Connection

Thyroid

Brain Connection

Headache

Spine II

Brain

Medulla Oblongata

Heart II

To my father for showing me the path, and my mother and husband for holding my hand every step of the way.

Made in United States
Troutdale, OR
01/03/2025

27589109R00031